The
WARLORD'S
ALARM

The
WARLORD'S
ALARM

By Virginia Walton Pilegard
Illustrated by Nicolas Debon

PELICAN PUBLISHING COMPANY
GRETNA 2006

*The word "Pelican" and the depiction of a pelican are trademarks
of Pelican Publishing Company, Inc., and are registered in the
U.S. Patent and Trademark Office.*

Library of Congress Cataloging-in-Publication Data

Pilegard, Virginia Walton.
  The warlord's alarm / by Virginia Walton Pilegard ; illustrated by Nicolas Debon.
    p. cm.
  Summary: While traveling to an important feast in ancient China, Chuan and
his friend Jing Jing devise a water "alarm" clock to make sure their party reaches
the emperor's palace before rival warlords. Includes a brief history of water clocks
and instructions for making one.
  ISBN-13: 978-1-58980-378-7 (alk. paper)
  [1. Time measurements—Fiction. 2. Clocks and watches—Fiction. 3. China—
History—To 221 B.C.—Fiction.] I. Debon, Nicolas, ill. II. Title.
  PZ7.P6283Wao 2006
  [E]—dc22
                          2006012496

Printed in Singapore
Published by Pelican Publishing Company, Inc.
1000 Burmaster Street, Gretna, Louisiana 70053

THE WARLORD'S ALARM

Many years ago in China, a young boy named Chuan and his friend Jing Jing set out on a journey to the city of the emperor. It was a time of unrest in the Middle Kingdom. The emperor had invited all of his military governors to a feast in order to determine which ones remained loyal to him. Ying-Fa, the powerful warlord with whom the children traveled, was eager to arrive before the others in order to gain the emperor's favor.

The days of marching stretched from the first rays of sunrise through midday, when Ying-Fa stopped to rest his horse, and ended when the shadows of evening joined together into darkness.

"Time passes slowly," Chuan grumbled.

"**E**ach day passes in the time it takes for my leather water bag to empty," said Jing Jing. "I fill it every morning and it leaks out through this tiny hole by nightfall." She wrung moisture from the bottom of her coat and made a face.

After some days they noticed more people on the road. Farmers trotted along, baskets swinging from their carrying poles. Carts heaped with vegetables rolled by. A rival warlord mounted on a fierce horse nodded at Ying-Fa as he passed and smiled a cold, haughty smile.

"I do not trust the *smiling one*," Ying-Fa said with a scowl. "He, too, travels to the emperor's feast. We are less than two days from the city. If he reaches the emperor first he will tell lies and spread mischief about me."

That evening found them nearing an inn already crowded with travelers—including the *smiling one.*

"We could ride all night and camp by the gates of the city," Chuan whispered to Ying-Fa. "That way you would be sure to be the first one to see the emperor."

"I will not be found camping like a beggar when guards open the gate to the City of Perpetual Peace." Ying-Fa stepped from his chariot. "When the gate opens tomorrow, I will ride through with dignity and you, clever Chuan, will see that we leave our beds in time."

The innkeeper's servant shoved Chuan and Jing Jing into a dark corner of a busy, smoke-filled room, where he brought them small bowls of tea and a meal of noodles and boiled cabbage.

"When must we leave here to reach the emperor's gates as they open?" Chuan asked the servant.

"One must leave this place four hours before the sun rises to stand before the emperor's guards when they swing open the city gates." The servant's mouth curled in a knowing sneer. "Sleep only half of the night or you will suffer your master's anger."

When the servant walked away, Chuan dropped his head into his hands. "Even if I sat up all night, I would not know *when* to wake Ying-Fa. An hour before sunrise I could look at the sky and see the light coming. But four hours? It is hopeless. And our master's temper is known even in this place."

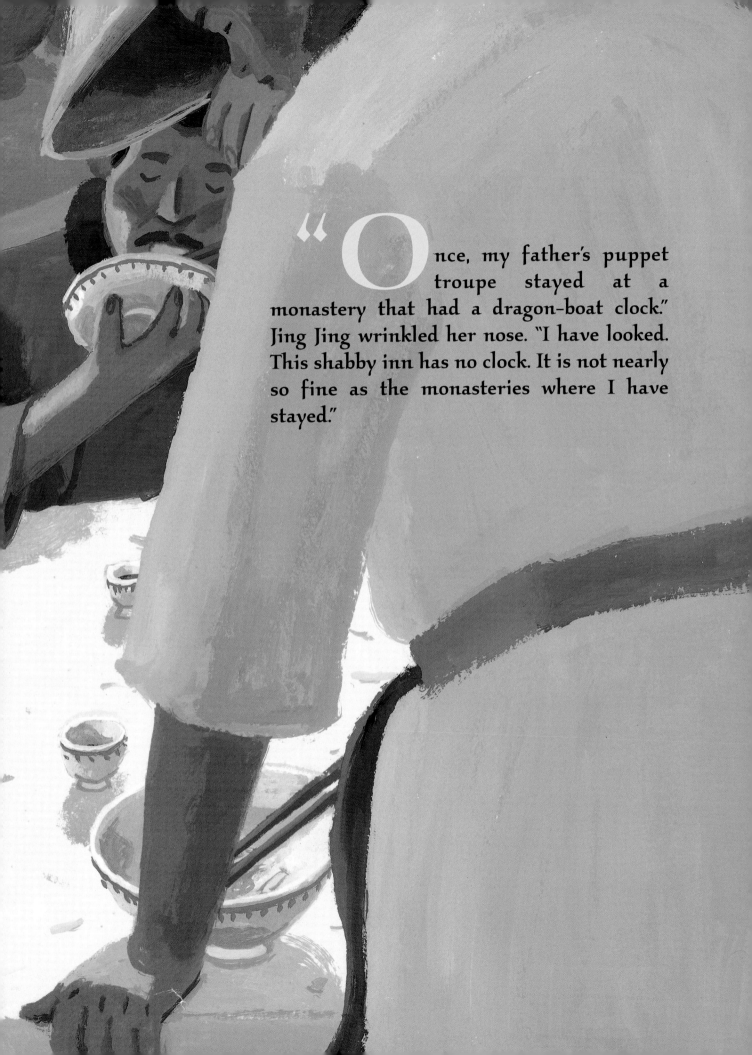

"Once, my father's puppet troupe stayed at a monastery that had a dragon-boat clock." Jing Jing wrinkled her nose. "I have looked. This shabby inn has no clock. It is not nearly so fine as the monasteries where I have stayed."

"**I** have never seen a clock," Chuan said, not raising his head. If he had not been so worried about failing the warlord, he would never have admitted that his friend knew more about some things than he did.

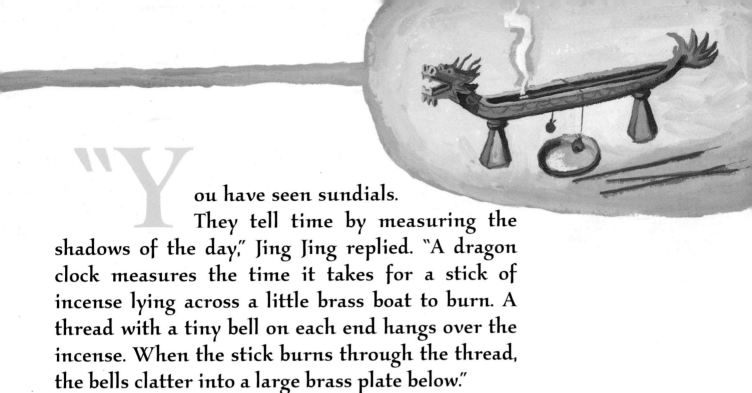

"Y ou have seen sundials. They tell time by measuring the shadows of the day," Jing Jing replied. "A dragon clock measures the time it takes for a stick of incense lying across a little brass boat to burn. A thread with a tiny bell on each end hangs over the incense. When the stick burns through the thread, the bells clatter into a large brass plate below."

"What is the use of your knowledge?" Chuan asked. "This lowly inn has neither bells, incense, nor brass dragon boats."

"I know that to tell time we must find something that happens again and again in a regular way. Shadows move in a regular way as the sun passes. Incense sticks burn in a regular way until they reach the string and the bells," Jing Jing said.

"I could tap my foot and you could keep count," Chuan suggested.

ing Jing yawned. "I don't think so," she said. "Besides, how many times would you have to tap to tell us the sun would rise in four hours?" She shrugged out of her wet coat and spread it out to dry. Wrapped in a quilt from their pack, she curled up on the hard floor. "A leaky water bag and no bed. Beds for our masters but no beds for us in this inadequate inn," she muttered.

Chuan jumped to his feet. He grabbed Jing Jing's water bag and held it high. Tiny drops of water fell onto the floor. "Your bag drips again and again in a regular way!"

Jing Jing rubbed her eyes and stared at the dripping water. "My bag leaks itself empty every day." She began to smile. "One whole bag, one whole day. Half a bag, half a day . . . or *night*. But, my friend, you are beginning to yawn too. How will you stay awake to watch the bag?"

Chuan rushed outside to fill the water bag. By the time he returned, he had an idea. With eager hands, he measured water into the dishes left from their dinner. The dish that had held noodles and cabbage held just less than half a bag of water. He poured the water back into the bag, and then poured in a little more from one of the other bowls.

While Jing Jing watched, Chuan set the empty dish on a shelf on the wall. Over it he hung the water bag to drip into the dish. He stretched out on the floor below the shelf.

"When the dripping water fills the bowl, the bowl will overflow on your head." Jing Jing clapped her hands. "How clever you are!"

It seemed the children had just fallen asleep when water began to splash onto Chuan's face. He awakened Jing Jing and they slipped through the dark inn to the place where Ying-Fa slept. In minutes the warlord's company assembled outside.

As the warlord had ordered, they
arrived at the city just when the
gates opened. They were swept along a grand,
wide avenue teeming with travelers with
exotic animals, circus performers, musicians,
and merchants selling every imaginable kind
of food and finery.

"I knew you would not disappoint me, clever Chuan," Ying-Fa said when at last they climbed the majestic steps of the imperial palace. "Remember to bow deeply in the presence of the emperor and be silent unless you are spoken to."

And so it was that Chuan, the resourceful peasant boy who had once known only the river where his father fished, entered with his friends into the presence of the revered emperor of all China.

You may have guessed that Chuan invented a type of alarm clock. History records an ancient Chinese water clock made by setting four copper kettles, one below another, on a stone staircase. Water from the top kettle dripped down through the second and third to the fourth kettle. It would take two hours for the full top kettle to empty into the second kettle. As water emptied from kettle to kettle, a servant held up a sign showing which *shi'chen* or two-hour interval had passed. When the water reached the bottom, the servant poured it into the top kettle to begin again.

In 1088, a three-story mechanical water clock more than thirty feet tall was built for China's emperor. The clock's top story had an armillary sphere for observing stars and planets. The middle story held a celestial globe to display their movements. Wooden puppets on the bottom story came out to strike a drum every fifteen minutes, ring a bell every hour, and beat a gong every two hours.

You can make your own water clock. Use a toothpick to make a tiny hole in the bottom of an eight-ounce Styrofoam cup. Suspend the cup over a glass quart jar and fill the cup with water. Cut a strip of cardboard and place it over one side of the top of the cup.

Tie a small bell to a two-inch cork, leaving about three inches of thread between the two. Balance the bell on the edge of the cardboard and float the cork in the water. In *time*, the water level in the cup will lower until the cork pulls the bell into the cup.

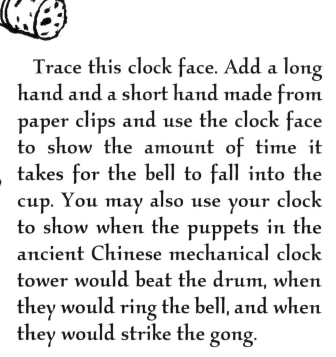

Trace this clock face. Add a long hand and a short hand made from paper clips and use the clock face to show the amount of time it takes for the bell to fall into the cup. You may also use your clock to show when the puppets in the ancient Chinese mechanical clock tower would beat the drum, when they would ring the bell, and when they would strike the gong.